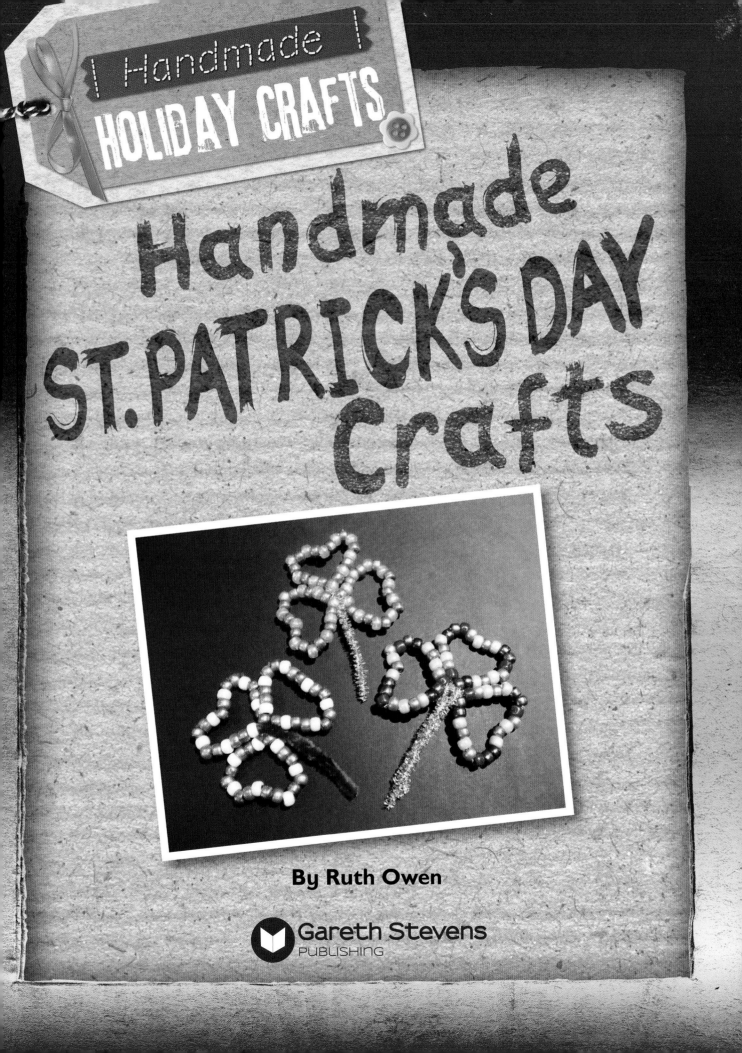

Handmade HOLIDAY CRAFTS

Handmade ST. PATRICK'S DAY Crafts

By Ruth Owen

Gareth Stevens
PUBLISHING

Please visit our website, www.garethstevens.com. For a free color catalog of all our high-quality books, call toll free 1-800-542-2595 or fax 1-877-542-2596.

Cataloging-in-Publication Data
Names: Owen, Ruth.
Title: Handmade St. Patrick's Day crafts / Ruth Owen.
Description: New York : Gareth Stevens Publishing, 2017. | Series: Handmade holiday crafts | Includes index.
Identifiers: ISBN 9781482460872 (pbk.) | ISBN 9781482461589 (library bound) | ISBN 9781482460889 (6 pack)
Subjects: LCSH: Saint Patrick's Day decorations--Juvenile literature. | Handicraft--Juvenile literature.
Classification: LCC TT900.S25 O84 2017 | DDC 745.594'166--dc23

Published in 2017 by
Gareth Stevens Publishing
111 East 14th Street, Suite 349
New York, NY 10003

First Edition

Produced for Gareth Stevens Publishing by Ruby Tuesday Books Ltd
Designer: Emma Randall

Photo Credits: Courtesy of Ruby Tuesday Books and Shutterstock.

Printed in the United States of America
CPSIA compliance information: Batch CW17GS.
For further information contact Gareth Stevens, New York, New York at 1-800-542-2595.

CONTENTS

A HAPPY HANDMADE HOLIDAY

When March 17 comes around, make sure you're ready to celebrate St. Patrick's Day and all its **traditions** with shamrocks, **leprechauns**, and pots of gold at the end of the rainbow.

Using some inexpensive craft supplies, **recycled** materials, and your own **creativity**, you can create fun decorations to get your home ready for the big day.

From beaded shamrocks to making leprechaun portraits of your family, just follow the step-by-step instructions to have a happy, handmade St. Patrick's Day.

STAY SAFE

It's very important to have an adult around whenever you do any of the following tasks:

- Use scissors
- Use wire cutters
- Use a glue gun

YOU WILL NEED:

To make the projects in this book, you don't need any special equipment—just some basic crafting tools and supplies.

- Scissors
- Glue gun
- White glue
- Paints and paintbrushes
- Stapler
- A black marker
- Glue stick
- A ruler
- A measuring tape

Happy St. Patrick's Day

BEADED SHAMROCK

The three-leaved shamrock is a **symbol** of Ireland and St. Patrick's Day. This first project shows you how to make a cute shamrock decoration using pipe cleaners and pony beads.

YOU WILL NEED:

- Pipe cleaners
- Pony beads in your choice of colors

1 To make each section of the shamrock, you will need 20 beads.

2 Take three pipe cleaners and thread 20 beads onto each one.

We chose a pattern of three alternating shades of green and blue.

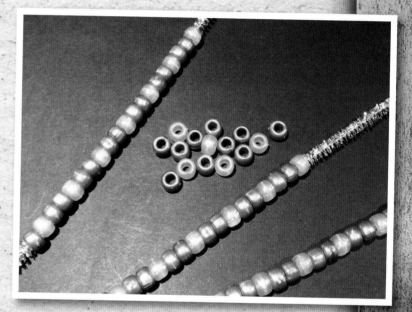

3 Now twist each pipe cleaner into a loop.

Next, twist two
of the beaded
loops together.

Then add the third
loop and tightly twist
its pipe cleaner into
the first two.

To make the shamrock's stem, either twist
or braid the pipe cleaners together.

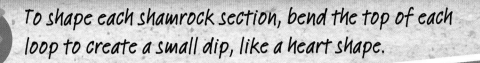

7 To shape each shamrock section, bend the top of each loop to create a small dip, like a heart shape.

Your lucky St. Patrick's Day shamrock is complete!

We also made shamrocks in green and the colors of Ireland's flag. Rainbows are also a St. Patrick's Day symbol, so we made a rainbow-colored shamrock, too.

This shamrock has a rainbow pattern of red, orange, yellow, green, blue, indigo, and violet.

Green is Ireland's national color.

The flag of Ireland has three vertical stripes in green, white, and orange.

ST. PATRICK'S DAY RIBBON

Have fun making this giant St. Patrick's Day ribbon, and **customize** it with beads and your own special greeting.

1 Take a sheet of green origami paper and fold it about six times into accordion folds, as follows.

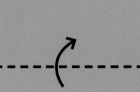

Fold up along the dotted line, and crease.

Turn the paper over and repeat.

Keep turning and folding.

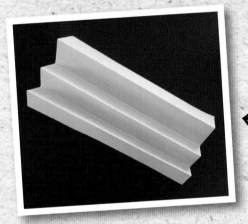

The paper should now look like this.

2 Repeat Step 1 with the other three sheets of green origami paper.

3 Take one folded piece of paper and close up the folds to form a thin strip. Then fold the strip in half to create a fan shape.

Join the two halves of the fan by stapling or gluing them.

Staple these two folds together.

Fold up the accordion strip of paper to create a fan shape.

4 Repeat with the other three folded pieces of paper.

5 Next, glue or staple the four fan sections together to create the ribbon.

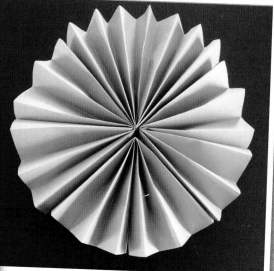

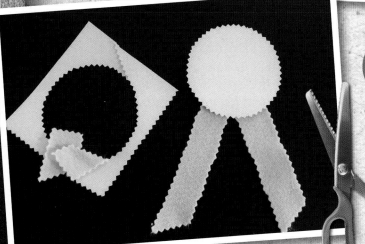

6 Make a circle of yellow cardboard for the center of your ribbon by placing a glass upside down on the cardboard and drawing around it. Then cut out the circle.

We used pinking shears to give the cardboard and felt a crinkly edge.

7 Cut two strips from the green felt and glue them to the back of the yellow circle.

8 Write your St. Patrick's Day greeting on the circle of yellow cardboard.

9 Then use the glue gun to glue the yellow cardboard to the green ribbon.

We used a green, white, and orange pattern—like the flag of Ireland.

10 To decorate your ribbon with beads, thread pony beads onto a pipe cleaner.

When the pipe cleaner is covered with beads, bend it into a circle that's the same size as the edge of the yellow cardboard. Twist the ends together and then trim off any spare pipe cleaner.

11 Use the glue gun to fix the beaded circle to the yellow cardboard.

12 Finally, cut a small piece of cardboard. Fix a safety pin to the cardboard with duct tape. Then glue the cardboard to the back of the ribbon.

Happy St. Patrick's Day!

LEPRECHAUN FAMILY PORTRAITS

On St. Patrick's Day, many people like to dress up as Irish fairy folk called leprechauns. Get busy with some photos and construction paper and make these fantastic leprechaun portraits of your family and friends!

YOU WILL NEED:

- Photographs
- Scissors
- Orange, green, black, and yellow construction paper
- A black and an orange marker
- A pencil
- A glue stick
- A small bowl
- A large piece of paper in your choice of color

Begin by taking photographs of your friends or family. Don't forget to take a selfie, too. Print out the photos.

Cut out the face from one of your photographs and lay it on the yellow paper.

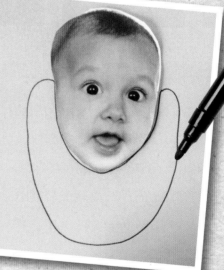 Draw a beard shape around the bottom half of the face.

Remove the face and then add a little extra section of beard so it will overlap the chin. Cut out the beard and flip it over so you can't see the black lines.

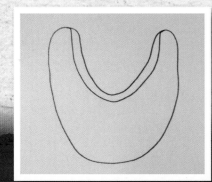

5 Now make the orange curls for your beard. Cut orange construction paper into thin strips. Take a strip and roll it tightly around a pencil. When you remove the coil of paper from the pencil, it will curl up.

6 Glue your paper curls to the yellow beard.

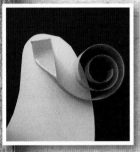   

7 To make a leprechaun hat, place the face on the green paper. Use an upturned bowl to draw a semicircle that's slightly larger than the person's head. Cut out the semicircle.

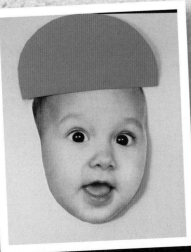

8 Now begin assembling your portrait. Glue the face to the top half of the large sheet of paper. Then glue on the top part of the hat.

9 Cut a thin strip of black paper that's the same width as the hat. Cut a thin strip of green paper that's wider than the hat. Glue both pieces to the picture.

10 To make a buckle for the hat, cut a small rectangle of yellow paper. Fold the rectangle in half, then cut a small rectangle from the center.

Glue the buckle to the picture.

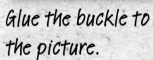

11 Draw on some orange hair at the sides of the face. Finally, glue on your curly leprechaun beard.

POT OF GOLD DECORATION

Old Irish **legends** say that leprechauns collect money and gold and hide it away. To trick humans who want to find their gold, leprechauns might say that their gold can be found at the end of a rainbow. Of course, however, everyone knows it's not possible to find the end of a rainbow!

YOU WILL NEED:

- Newspaper
- Black and gold spray paint
- Some pebbles or stones
- A terra-cotta flowerpot
- Popsicle sticks
- Paints and paintbrushes
- A pencil
- Scissors
- White cardboard
- A glue gun
- Cotton balls
- White glue

1 Collect pebbles and chunks of stone to be your nuggets of gold. You will need enough to fill the flowerpot.

Make sure you ask permission before taking stones from a garden.

2 Place the stones on some newspaper. Spray them with gold paint so each stone is completely covered, and allow to dry thoroughly.

When using spray paint, open a window and make sure the room is well ventilated with plenty of fresh air.

3 Stand the flowerpot on another piece of newspaper. Spray it with the black paint inside and out, and allow to dry thoroughly.

4 Next, paint seven popsicle sticks in the colors of the rainbow.

Red
Orange
Yellow
Green
Blue
Indigo
Violet

5 Draw a cloud shape on the white cardboard and cut it out.

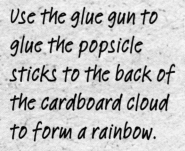

6 Use the glue gun to glue the popsicle sticks to the back of the cardboard cloud to form a rainbow.

7 Spread white glue over the front of the cardboard cloud and then cover it with torn up cotton balls.

8 Use the glue gun to glue the popsicle stick rainbow and cloud to the inside upper edge of the painted flowerpot.

9 Then fill the flowerpot with your gold pebbles, so it is almost overflowing.

Your gold at the end of the rainbow is ready to decorate your home for St. Patrick's Day!

RAINBOW GARLAND

Celebrate St. Patrick's Day by decorating your home with this fantastic rainbow garland made from thick paper or thin card stock. Once you get folding, you won't want to stop!

YOU WILL NEED:

- Thick construction paper or thin card stock in rainbow colors
- A ruler
- Scissors
- A glue stick

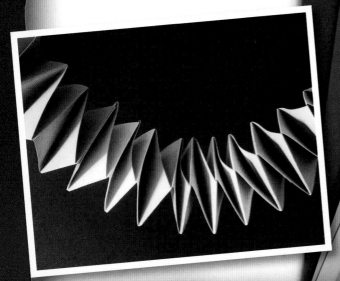

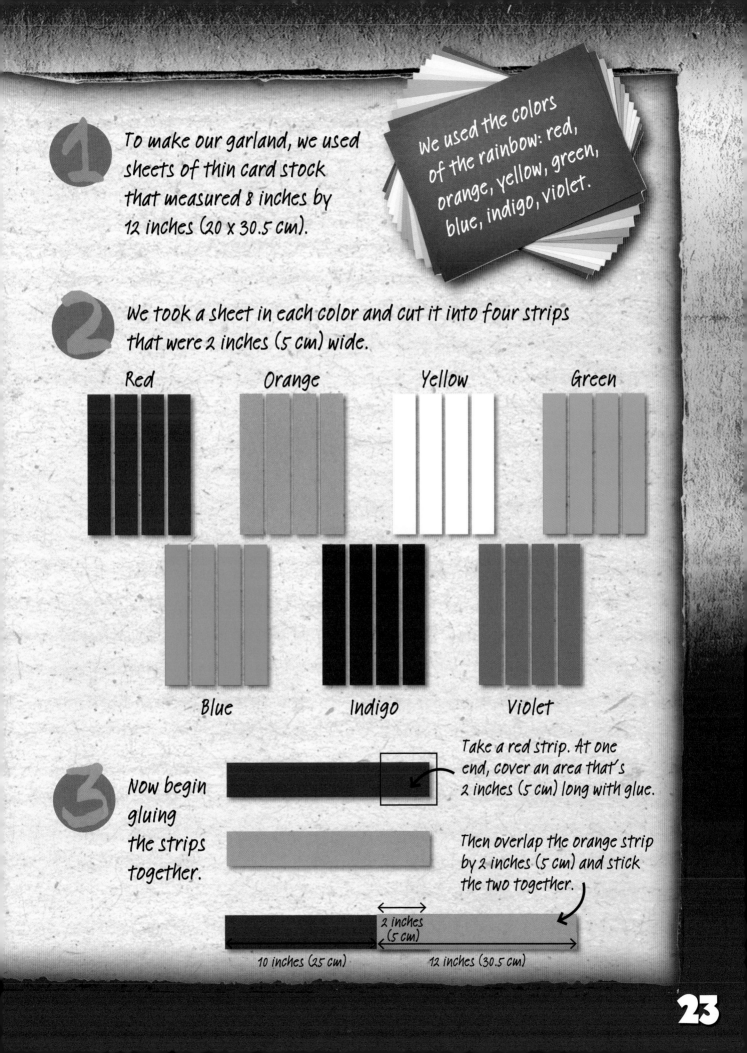

1 To make our garland, we used sheets of thin card stock that measured 8 inches by 12 inches (20 x 30.5 cm).

We used the colors of the rainbow: red, orange, yellow, green, blue, indigo, violet.

2 We took a sheet in each color and cut it into four strips that were 2 inches (5 cm) wide.

Red   Orange   Yellow   Green

Blue   Indigo   Violet

3 Now begin gluing the strips together.

Take a red strip. At one end, cover an area that's 2 inches (5 cm) long with glue.

Then overlap the orange strip by 2 inches (5 cm) and stick the two together.

2 inches (5 cm)

10 inches (25 cm)   12 inches (30.5 cm)

Keep gluing strips together following the colors of the rainbow until you have 14 strips in a long strand.

5 Then repeat to create a second long strand with the other 14 strips.

6 To combine the two strands, you will need a large work surface such as a table or kitchen countertop. Or you can work on the floor on a hard surface.

 Two strands that each contain 14 strips will make a garland that's 4 feet (1.2 m) long.

7 Glue the ends of the two long strands together to form a right angle, as shown. They should overlap by 2 inches (5 cm).

8 Now fold down the top (purple) strand, and crease hard.

9 Next, fold the strand that's on the right-hand side (red) over the other strand (purple), and crease hard.

10 Fold up the bottom strand (purple), and crease hard.

11 Next, fold over the left-hand strand (red), and crease hard.

You can see the folds of the garland forming.

12 To complete your garland, keep folding the two strands together until all the paper is folded.

If you want to make a longer garland, repeat all the steps and then glue the two garlands together.

ST. PATRICK'S DAY RAG WREATH

Get your home ready for St. Patrick's Day by making this handmade rag door wreath. Scraps of green felt and fabric, ribbons, and even old clothes can all be used to make this project.

YOU WILL NEED:

- Fabric and ribbon
- A measuring tape
- Scissors
- Thick wire or a wire coat hanger
- Wire cutters
- Duct tape
- Piece of ribbon for hanging

1 Begin by selecting your fabrics or ribbons. You can buy squares of fabric for quilting from craft stores.

You can also recycle by cutting up old items such as clothes, tablecloths, or cushion covers.

Quilting squares

Recycled fabrics

2 Cut your choice of fabrics into strips that are about 6 inches (15 cm) long and 1.5 inches (4 cm) wide. You will need about 100 strips to make the wreath.

3 To make the frame for the wreath, bend a length of wire into a circle that has a diameter of about 8 inches (20 cm) across.

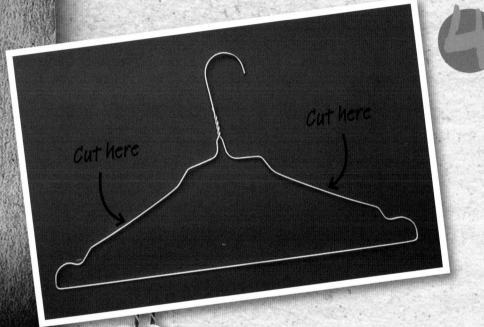

Cut here

Cut here

4 If you're using a wire coat hanger, ask an adult to help you cut off the hooked part using wire cutters. Then bend the wire into a circle. Don't worry if it's not a perfectly round circle—it won't show under the fabric.

When cutting and bending wire, be careful of any sharp edges on the ends of the wire.

5 Use duct tape to tape the ends of the circle of wire together. Then wrap the wire circle with duct tape.

6 Begin tying the fabric strips to the wreath frame. All you need to do is tie each strip in a single tight knot.

7 You can tie strips alongside each other and on top of each other.

8 Keep adding strips to the wreath. Push them together on the frame so they are bunched tightly together.

Don't worry if any pieces of fabric look frayed. It all adds to the handmade effect of the wreath.

This is a fun project to make with friends or family. Have everyone help cut fabric strips or tie them into the wreath.

9 When your wreath is complete, tie on a piece of ribbon for hanging and place the wreath on your door.

GLOSSARY

creativity
The use of imagination or original ideas to create something new and unusual.

customize
Change or add decorations to something so that it is one of a kind, or unique.

legends
Stories handed down from long ago that are often based on some facts but cannot be proven to be true.

leprechauns
Fairy folk that appear in Irish legends. Leprechauns are said to look like tiny men with orange or red beards and green suits and hats.

recycled
Objects or materials that have been turned into something new instead of being thrown away.

symbol
An object or picture that stands for or represents another thing. For example, a shamrock shape is a symbol of Ireland.

traditions
Ways of thinking, behaving, or doing something that a group of people have followed for a long time. For example, dressing up as leprechauns is traditional on St. Patrick's Day.

INDEX

FURTHER INFORMATION

BOOKS:

Holm, Sharon. *Crafts for St. Patrick's Day.* Minneapolis, MN: Millbrook Press, 2012.

Malaspina, Ann. *St. Patrick's Day Crafts.* North Mankato, MN: Child's World, 2016.

WEBSITES:

http://www.freekidscrafts.com/holidays/st-patricks-day-crafts/
Visit here for more St. Patrick's Day crafts, including hats, wreaths, accessories, and more.